Autumn Nature Activities for Chilc

Irmgard Kutsch and Brigitte Walden

Autumn Nature Activities for Children

Floris Books

Translated by Ronald E. Koetzsch

First published in German in 2001 as *Natur-Kinder-Garten-Werkstatt:*
Herbst, by Verlag Freies Geistesleben, Stuttgart

First published in English in 2005 by Rudolf Steiner College Press,
California and Floris Books, Edinburgh
Second printing 2010

Publication of this book has been made possible by a grant from the
Waldorf Curriculum Fund

British Library CIP Data available

ISBN 978-086315-495-9

Printed in China

NOVEMBER (Part 2)

Foreword

I saw Irmgard Kutsch for the first time at a workshop, and she was very much in her element. She sat at a spinning wheel and let the fluffy wool pass through her fingers. The forming of the yarn seemed effortless. Sometimes it was thin and fine, sometimes thick and knotty, as the natural material allowed, but always full of life. Irmgard Kutsch sat there and radiated the joy and calm of a person who is totally in harmony with her craft. Quite spontaneously, I had a feeling that this is something good; this woman lives what she teaches.

Her joy was communicated effortlessly and with few words. The children pressed close to her and, quite entranced, tried to bring the simple spindle into movement or to weave the wool on the little wooden frames. The adults also tried and often quickly noticed that it was not as easy as it looked to find the necessary gentle, natural rhythm. Has it been lost in a society that hardens us for competition?

It became clear for me, on this sunny day in May, just how important the work of the Children's Nature and Garden Centre is. Children want to, and should, experience the world with all their senses, with body and soul. Only when they are securely connected to the earth, well grounded in wholesome physical and spiritual experiences, will they later be able to deal with the world of illusion they find on computer and television screens.

I think it's very important that Irmgard Kutsch and Brigitte Walden — through this series of books — can share their experiences at the Children's Nature and Garden Centre with many open-minded early childhood educators. There cannot be enough people who acquaint children with the roots of life. Something so good should touch as many people as possible.

Today, books often play the role of cultural transmitter. The natural chain of transmission frequently broken: in earlier times, children learned in their everyday life — from grandmothers and grandfathers as well as parents — how to deal with nature and how to work with their hands. They learned how to make a fire, fetch water, care for animals, sow and harvest, store food and bake bread.

In my generation it had already changed, but I was fortunate. I had a grandmother who gave me both a love of gardening and the courage to write. In her garden, I was always free just to be there. Those memories have stayed with me all my life: the scent of elderberries; the radiant yellow marigolds; the mighty rhubarb bushes; the big old apple tree; the rich loamy soil; the shining buttercups; picking beans and pressing sauerkraut. The roots of a love of gardening can start to grow even in childhood. Later, in my parents' garden, I was allowed to try out anything I wanted. For me it was a safe and love-imbued world, full of deeply meaningful experiences.

It was probably much the same for Irmgard Kutsch and Brigitte Walden. And so we pass on our treasured experiences to a new generation that has grown up without their own apple tree and without a fire in the stove.

Through her work and her books, Irmgard Kutsch has become a kind of Super Grandmother who has filled the gap between the generations. She is helping insecure children of the twenty-first century to keep their feet on the ground. Only someone who has the opportunity to get

very close to nature can really learn to love it. And the person who loves the earth will appreciate and protect it.

In this, the *Autumn* volume of the Nature Activities for Children series, children and educators will learn how to grow and work with their own vegetables and make them into delicious, healthy meals. Potatoes do not come out of a plastic bag in the supermarket but out of the moist brown earth. There is a big difference.

Late in autumn, we gather roots and grasses and cut branches. In basket-making, an ancient skill is reawakened. Before winter comes, children will learn what it means to have a protecting roof over their heads: to be safe and secure in a pleasant place; to feel at home. Building a house has always been an elemental and necessary activity all over the world. A house you build yourself outdoors brings a totally different set of feelings and experiences from those of an apartment with concrete walls and plastic windows which blank out the environment.

In the dark, cold time of the year, light and warmth have a special meaning. The light and warmth that stream from a beeswax candle you have dipped yourself create warm feelings. This is totally different from experiencing the light that comes invisibly and anonymously out of an electric socket in the wall. The fragrant wax carries the memory of the flower-filled summer and the industrious life of the bees.

In this book, many activities are presented for practical instruction, and philosophical or educational growth. The ideas and the evocative, lively photographs inspire us to participate in the same experiences and feelings. That is the aim. The Children's Nature and Garden Centre welcomes everyone who wants to join in.

I sincerely hope that Irmgard Kutsch and Brigitte Walden will reach many people through their valuable work and lively books, and make many children happy.

Marie-Louise Kreuter,
author of gardening books

The Story of this Series of Books

Encouraging children's love of exploration

This is two-year-old Saskia. Like almost all children of this age, she has a deep interest in the natural world. She has worked tirelessly now for two hours, picking up apples from underneath the apple tree, bringing them one by one to the water bucket, and washing them. She has discovered to her surprise that, although she carefully dunks them again and again into the water, they never stay on the bottom but come back stubbornly to the top. This gives her great pleasure and motivates her to try again with one apple after another.

The newly fallen apples give off such a delicious aroma that Saskia feels invited to take a bite out of one, and then another. The sour taste is not very nice, so she turns her attention to the next shining green-gold candidate. Again and again, she takes an apple in both hands and, from a short distance, throws it into the water bucket where it lands with a dull splash among the other apples.

She totters with a hurried step over the bumpy ground of the garden, and her muscles and her sense of balance must work hard to stop her from falling down. Finally her socks and sweater have become so wet that, despite her loud protests, her mother calls Saskia away from this activity that she chose herself, and that has held her attention.

The variety of sensory perceptions and of possibilities for sense development in this scenario are actually much greater than what is described here. From this engrossing activity, Saskia has a fresh, healthy glow in her cheeks, and her hands and feet — despite the work in cold water — are snugly warm afterward, almost glowing. And so much exercise in the fresh air brings a hearty appetite. Saskia sits down to eat, a little tired — as might be expected — and regains the energy she has exuberantly expended. Time for a nap in her cozy bed, where she has a deep sleep. After so much activity, one needs a little rest.

This scene is one of many that have shown me how important life in and with nature is for child development. I see this especially in my work in kindergartens and special schools for children with developmental problems. Being outside, in nature, has a harmonizing effect. In nature, adults have many opportunities to offer children examples of life's interrelationships, and to give them seminal experiences by which they can orient themselves in life.

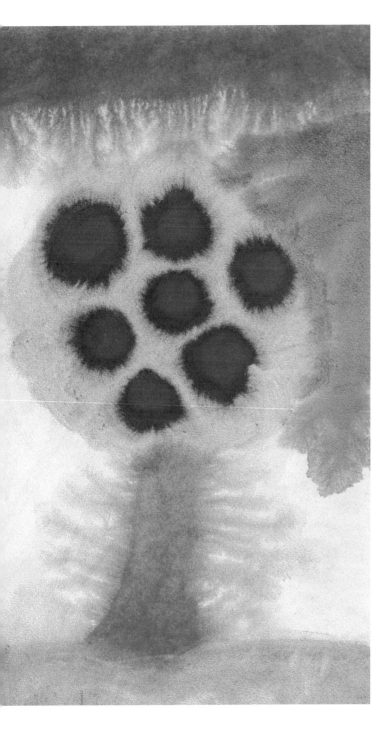

The four books in this series each deal with one season of the year. They are to help adults who want to foster healthy child development through nature experiences in daycare centres, playgroups, early childhood programmes, kindergartens, primary schools, in work with children with disabilities, and also within the family. In each activity, we introduce the children to different seasonal aspects of nature. Each volume in the series stands alone and can be used without reference to the others.

The Children's Nature and Garden Centre in Reichshof, Germany

How will our world look in twenty to thirty years? What are the skills that the children of today, even in their early years, will have to develop in order to be able to create a future that is worth living and worthy of love?

These questions led Irmgard Kutsch to establish the Children's Nature and Garden Centre of Reichshof in 1994. In her almost thirty years of nature-oriented work with children, adolescents and adults, she observed the growing numbers of children with problems in development, sensory perception and movement, and with severe behavioral difficulties. One reason for this is because children live in a deluding, virtual world of television and computer-screen images, and so they can receive experiences only through their visual and auditory senses. True contact with the world, however, can be achieved only by active involvement in the world.

Understanding through hands-on activities

A parallel development is that destruction of nature has gone so far, that people need to take responsibility for creating a new ecological culture.

The work in the Children's Nature and Garden Centre focuses on human beings here and now, and the way we interact with the world. This is based on the natural world and its yearly passage through the seasons.

In the centre of all this is the child with his or her natural needs: the instinct for play; the joy in experimentation; the impulse to movement. In an atmosphere of love and protection, a child can trust adults who behave thoughtfully and consciously. A child can develop both a basic scientific understanding of the world and the foundation for an all-embracing interest in the world.

Therefore, in the Children's Nature and Garden Centre, understanding is communicated directly through practical activities for children and adults of all ages. The themes relate to particular regions but also to trans-regional culture and history. By consciously bringing in intercultural aspects and including artistic activities, the work is contemporary but also for the future. The children learn to live with one another, accepting and respecting different religions and cultures.

The next generation can be helped today by a network of knowledgeable and capable teachers: to go beyond an isolated existence in kindergarten and elementary school, and to help create a new social culture. When children and adolescents can

find in adults' perception, thinking, and behaviour a viable standard that can act as a model for them, this can help prevent violence in the future. A comprehensive child health programme can also protect against later drug use.

Conscious, loving adults provide an example that awakens joy and interest in imitating conscious activity. This also awakens imaginative self-expression and creativity. It brings a positive attitude toward work and contributes to an education that fosters ecological and social awareness.

Irmgard Kutsch

11

SEPTEMBER

Harvesting fruit and vegetables

Black-eyed Susan, a typical late summer and autumn flower

Everything in nature conceals a secret

Under the sign of Virgo (the Virgin), the exuberance of high summer gradually fades in the natural world. The flow of sap in the plants decreases. The fullness of summer comes to an end as the sun sinks lower and fruits ripen. In the ripening seeds and swelling fruit, the plant concentrates the light and warmth of summer.

Many flowering bushes take on warm brown, red and yellow tones. On September 23, the sun passes into Libra (the Scales) and the autumnal equinox arrives. For migratory birds, it is a sign to head south.

In this time of plenty, many animals such as the squirrel create stockpiles for the cold, barren season ahead. It is also a time for people to harvest the crops that were sown in the spring. Most of our local fruits and vegetables are ripe now.

Where Do Fruit and Vegetables Come from?

Some of us are blessed to live in prosperity and security, where there is an abundance of what we need. We are used to always having exactly what we want. Wherever you look, there are supermarkets with food from many different countries — particularly in the fruit and vegetable section. Let's follow the steps in production and transportation of the products that end up in our shopping basket.

Many imported foods come from countries where poverty and hunger prevail. This applies, for example, to bananas. Through the insatiable consumption of the rich nations, the food supply of the poor nations is destroyed. Over-eating in industrialized countries causes malnutrition in the third world.

We need to create an alternative to the marketplace that overflows with products that are detrimental to the healthy development of all humankind. We also need to create an alternative to the principle of free market competition that often leads to oppression and destruction. We need a selection of goods produced in harmony with the laws and processes of nature. We can try to be independent of huge corporations and supermarkets and can boycott food and animal feed products from countries where there is an inadequate food supply.

There are positive signs of change. More and more conventional farmers are recognizing the colossal damage to the environment of large-scale animal farming and monoculture. Increasing numbers of farms and gardens have converted to more natural methods of producing basic foods such as fruit, vegetables, eggs, milk and grains.

Biodynamic Farms and the Environment

This sugar beet lantern was made at a harvest festival on a biodynamic farm

The feed for animals raised on biodynamic farms is predominantly grown on the farm itself. (Biodynamic agriculture is a type of organic agriculture based on the work of Rudolf Steiner.) The fertilizer for meadows, pasture land, and for grain and vegetable fields comes from carefully tended compost piles, which use the manure from the animals on the farm and are allowed to mature over several years. Thus a biodynamic farm is a self-contained agricultural organism.

These farms do not see themselves only as places of food production. Much more than that, they are concerned about caring for the earth and for the small and even microscopic organisms that inhabit it. This leads to a healthy and productive natural environment. The interplay of earth, water, air, light, and even the influence of the stars, is considered in all phases of the agricultural process from sowing to harvesting. Today we must dust off the old traditions that contain wisdom about the relationships in nature, and reconsider them with a clear, contemporary and critical consciousness.

A strong cultural impulse radiates from these organic and biodynamic farms. Interested cus-

We can be thankful and happy when everything has grown as well as the vegetables on this harvest wagon

tomers form associations to support the farms and consider themselves to be more than just consumers. They feel responsible for the growth and care of the cultivated food products, and for the domestic animals. Many city-dwellers find these activities deeply satisfying, and a healthy balance to office work and city life.

Biodynamic farmers, in addition to the demanding work of farming, contribute to cultural life by offering lectures and tours of the fields and barns. People come from far and wide to experience annual festivals on the farm. Food takes on a new meaning; it has a higher value than mere survival. Children and adults can experience how demanding and labour-intensive ecological farming is: fewer machines are used and more work is done by hand. They realize that the farmer is always looking out for his crop and keeping an eye on weather conditions such as excessive rain, cold, storms, hail, drought or premature frost.

Natural Wholefoods in the Kindergarten

These natural alternatives in agriculture are especially interesting to daycare facilities, kindergartens and schools, if wholefoods are going to be provided to the children. Teacher training and parenting classes can involve not only the farmers and the proprietors of wholefood shops but also nutritionists and physicians who are acquainted with natural medicine. A concern for nutrition is essential to a holistic approach to health. Every individual educator who is entrusted with the care of children should have the help of specialists in providing a holistic approach to health.

In any case, it is important that healthy foods at breakfast, lunch and snack times be part of the practice of a kindergarten. This may be an additional factor for parents to consider when deciding on a kindergarten.

Whether a change to wholesome meals can be accomplished lies, first of all, with the head teacher. If the head teacher is committed to the idea and sees the preparation and presentation of food as an enriching educational activity, then those actually preparing the food will go along with it.

➤ The Healthy Foods Initiative in Wiesbaden

The city of Wiesbaden in Germany has more than 2000 children between the age of two and twelve in its municipal childcare centres. It offers at least one hot, freshly prepared meal every day. The basic principles of this initiative are as follows:

* emphasize vegetables
* use foods that are as natural (fresh and whole) as possible without unnecessary processing
* use raw vegetables or fruit for about half of the meal
* avoid preservatives and other additives
* buy organically-certified foods
* buy fruit and vegetables from local producers
* create balanced and varied menus of whole grain products, vegetables, fruit, potatoes, beans, milk, milk products and small quantities of fish, meat and eggs
* prepare the meals with both taste and appearance in mind, and serve them in a visually attractive way

These principles have been successfully implemented due to the nutritional and environmental awareness of teachers and childcare providers. Continuing education courses were used to gradually build up awareness. They included:

* a presentation by the German Institute for Nutrition
* a report by the Research Institute for Childhood Nutrition
* a visit to the homemakers' association of the state of Hessen
* meat: pros and cons
* healthy local food products
* a tour of a whole grain bakery
* protein requirements for a healthy diet
* Christmas baking with honey and herbs

These large pumpkins have taken a long time to grow. The children have often visited and been amazed by them. Now they will be made into delicious pumpkin soup and jolly lanterns.

* the pleasure of whole grain baking through the year
* a visit to a store with environmentally friendly products
* ecology education and healthy nutrition
* consequences of over-eating
* allergies and eating disorders
* a visit to a food-processing centre
* grading and hygienic handling of food
* herbs: their composition, effects and use; a visit to a medicinal herb garden

All of this in-service training, available for many years, was also attended by the schools' kitchen staff. In order to achieve the ideal of having healthy meals in the childcare centres, all employees received education and training and had to meet qualification standards. Funding was available to all personnel for this training.

Multicultural cooking festivals were also celebrated by all the childcare facilities. Here, food truly became an expression of love. The city of Wiesbaden is now associated with healthy food.

We have described the results of Wiesbaden's many years of effort to institute a healthy nutrition programme in its childcare centres in the hope that this information can be used in other places to influence political leaders, officials and parents. We hope that such a programme for wholesome, natural foods will become an accepted element in all kindergartens and childcare facilities.

The general initiative began with a programme whose motto was "vegetables instead of grass." Teachers and children planted vegetables in little gardens and in raised beds. The process led, of course, to harvesting and eating. The everyday experience of eating was placed in its ecological context. For the children it meant that, rather than

Teachers learn to recognize herbs and vegetables at the Children's Nature and Garden Centre

being merely consumers, they actively participated in the production and preparation of their own food.

Local people, including parents of the children, were then hired to make freshly prepared meals from the harvest. Through this, the children could see how a meal came into being, and could enjoy food of higher quality. For the parents there was an economic benefit: the cost of meals at the centre went down.

There are other similar examples of attempts to make nutrition an important element in education. The following sections contain practical information for those wanting to follow a similar model.

The Children's House in Siegen

Here, three meals a day are offered:

Breakfast only	$20 per week
Breakfast and lunch	$70 per week
Breakfast, lunch and afternoon snack	$75 per week

Every day, forty wholefood lunches are prepared in large pots on a stove. An oven is used if necessary. There is a storeroom for vegetables, fruit and bread and a refrigerator for dairy products. Two part-time cooks work ten hours per week and are paid from the money received for meals. The head of the kitchen orders what is in season and available from farmers in the area. Imported items are avoided as much as possible. Most food is bought directly from the farmers. Supplemental items are purchased at natural food stores.

Care is taken to minimize waste. For this reason, the children receive small portions and can then take a second helping. The social value of food and eating is emphasized. Breakfast preparation is seen as an important aspect of the educational process. Meals are eaten together at a large table.

The Integrated Childcare Centre in Siegen

All seventy children receive three wholefood meals a day. The monthly cost is about $90. The cook is a part-time employee paid about $16,000 per year. The kitchen was added when the facility was being renovated.

The kitchen is located in the basement. The cook is happy to open the window during the children's play time so they can look in and see what is being prepared for them.

As a part of the mealtime routine here, each child receives a cloth napkin in a napkin holder that has his or her name on it.

The Waldorf Kindergarten in Dortmund-Benninghofen

All fifteen children receive three wholefood meals a day here. The cost is about $75 per month. The cook comes in for two hours a day. The preparation of breakfast is part of the children's morning activity.

Here a mealtime ritual is observed. A blessing is said before the meal, and there is a shared beginning and end to the meal.

Information and Advice

If a childcare provider or kindergarten teacher wants to change from packaged snacks and prepared foods to natural wholefoods, Waldorf kindergartens can provide advice and help. For decades, the preparation of healthy meals, eaten

Looking, smelling, tasting and touching – every day, children in a Waldorf kindergarten enjoy basic sense experiences in preparing fresh foods

Freshly harvested herbs are processed by the children

together, has been part of the Waldorf educational approach. The Waldorf movement understands that the preparation of healthy foods is closely connected to a wholesome enjoyment of life and of the world. Natural food consultants and healthfood store owners can also be helpful.

The kindergarten in Siegen reports that the dentist, on making his annual visit, was surprised by the healthy teeth of the children in the kindergarten. Nowadays, as a result of eating sugared foods, most children today have serious tooth decay problems — their teeth sometimes even turning black.

It is important for the health of the coming generation that they recognize that food is life-giving. This insight can be offered to children as something obvious. Moreover, kindergartens implementing a natural foods programme are favourite customers of organic farms and natural food shops: they're regulars, and thus can usually get the best produce — for example, freshly picked vegetables, fresh-baked bread, fresh milk, yogurt and so on — delivered each week. Anyone accepting and supporting these ideas will gain a new appreciation of food which can be passed on to the children.

Eating Together:
A Good Influence

From our years of experience in the kindergarten, we can say that certain basic principles must be implemented. For example, new eating habits are more easily developed when all the kindergarten meals are prepared with the children.

At festival times, the meal should reflect the meaning of the holiday and should be clearly something special. Imagination can be given free rein. Cultural life can express itself even in the rituals of mealtime.

When there are children from ethnic minorities and from other countries in the kindergarten, it is important that their festivals are celebrated, and that food from their culture is included. This will make both the children and their parents feel more accepted and at home. It will also give the other children a valuable experience of another culture. In a multicultural world, one needs a broad perspective. A multicultural world can grow into an intercultural society.

After we have thought about what to eat, we must consider how we will eat it. This is also an educational issue that has to do with the cultural practices we want to develop in the children:

❀ eating together at one large table
❀ setting the table and decorating it together
❀ serving the meal that has been prepared together
❀ saying a grace or blessing the meal
❀ dividing up the work of clearing the table, washing up and putting things away

At a young age, children can begin to share in meaningful, appropriate work in the kitchen

By imitation, by repeating the blessing verse every day, children begin to sense that the beautiful sounds and rhymes bring a rich inner nourishment to open and expectant souls. Also, they are receiving, without realizing it, an effective training in good articulation, particularly if the adults speak the verse clearly, beautifully and with joy.

Understanding How Things Are Connected: Training the Senses

When children are involved in harvesting and preparing vegetables and fruit, especially from their own garden, they experience in the best possible way the interrelationships and processes of human life and nature. Through the work itself, their senses are enriched and trained, and their motor coordination is developed. For example, in many kindergartens one can harvest apples from a tree on the property or in a nearby garden. Many delicious things can be made from the apples.

In the early autumn, we gather the abundance of the summer and work with it so that it will keep through the autumn and winter. The children are delighted when, during the cold months, they find fruit that they harvested and processed months earlier reappearing on special occasions in yogurt, muesli, birthday cake, as jam on bread or as a piece of dried fruit. The next section contains basic recipes.

When children have all been involved in the preparation of the meal, it is nice to eat together at one table

Pictures on the right — clockwise from top left:

Because of their thorns, blackberries are plants that children will treat with great respect. Picking the delicious fruit helps develop fine motor skills and hand-eye coordination.

Working with their father, the children press fresh apples.

Harvesting of "box-potatoes." In kindergartens with limited space, these boxes give children an opportunity to experience cultivation of potatoes from the planting of the sprout right through to the harvest.

When fruit is processed right after picking, children can experience the true flavour and aroma.

Recipes for Freshly-Harvested Fruit

— Baked apples

Use one large apple per person. Core the apples almost all the way through, leaving a little of the apple at the bottom to make a cavity. Fill the cavity with nuts, honey and cinnamon, and top with a pat of butter. Bake in a buttered pan with a little water for about 2 hours at F 325°/150°C or until the apples are tender. They taste particularly delicious baked on an open fire.

— Jam from fresh fruit

1¹/₂ pounds (750 g) fresh fruit
¹/₂ pound (250 g) honey
Add 1–3 teaspoons of pectin if needed for thickening

The Apple

1. With - in a lit - tle ap - ple so co - sy and so small there are five lit - tle cham - bers a - round a lit - tle hall.
2. In ev' - ry room are sleep - ing two seeds of gold - en brown. They're ly - ing there and dream - ing in beds of ei - der - down.
3. They're dream - ing there of sun - shine and how it's going to be, when they shall hang as ap - ples up - on a Christ - mas tree.

Lyre ostinato   *Ending*

Mix washed, cut-up fruit with the honey and pectin and heat, stirring constantly, not over F110°/40°C. Let it stand and thicken for about 10 minutes. Fill jars with the jam and put them in the refrigerator. The jam keeps for three to four weeks. To keep for longer, sterilize the jars and seal them.

⌐ Jam for the winter larder

2 pounds (1 kg) fruit
1¹/2 pounds (750 g) granulated/preserving sugar

Wash the fruit and remove seeds and stones. Cut into small pieces. Put into a large, shallow saucepan and slowly bring to the boil. Gradually add the sugar. Cook, stirring, for about thirty minutes until enough liquid has boiled off to thicken the jam. Test on a spoon for thickness and taste. Pour the hot jam into hot sterilized jars with screw tops.

⌐ Jelly from fruit juice

Mix 2 pounds (1 kg) (about 6 US cups) of fruit juice and 2 pounds (1 kg) of granulated/preserving sugar in a heavy saucepan. Cook for four minutes at a rolling boil. Put in warm, dry, sterilized glasses and seal.

⌐ Cake with seasonal fruit

¹/2 pound (200 g) butter
4 ounces (100 g) (¹/2 US cup) sugar
lemon
oil
2 eggs
¹/2 pound (200 g) (1¹/4 US cup) fresh ground whole-wheat flour
2 teaspoons baking powder

(For 25 children, double the recipe)

Mix all the ingredients thoroughly and put the batter in a greased baking tin. Decorate the top with pieces of fruit. Bake for 45 minutes at F350°/180°C.

⌐ Fruit juice from steamed fruit

10 pounds (4 kg) fruit
1 pound (400 g) sugar

Wash the fruit. Put it in the basket of a steamer and sprinkle with sugar. Fill the lower section with 1 quart (1 litre) of water. Cover and bring to the boil. Over a moderate heat the fruit yields its juice in about an hour. Pour the juice into warm, sterilized bottles and seal immediately.

⌐ Apple pancakes   (20 children)

To make the batter: mix together 1 pound (400 g) of fresh ground whole-wheat flour, four eggs, a quart (1 litre) of milk, and 2 teaspoons of salt.

   Core 1 pound (500 g) of apples and cut into small pieces. Put a little oil in a hot frying pan, then a ladle of batter. Sprinkle with apple pieces. Flip the pancake after a few minutes to cook the other side.

⌐ Yogurt herb salad dressing   (25 children)

1 pound (500 g) plain natural yogurt (you could use quark if available)
1 teaspoon salt
1 tablespoon sugar (UK tablespoon = 1¹/3 US tablespoon)
juice of 2 lemons

Take a small amount of each of the herbs available in the garden: for example, three sprigs of parsley, ten chive stalks, a little cress and so on. Wild herbs, such as dandelion or stinging nettle, are also excellent. Finely cut the herbs. Mix all the ingredients in a large bowl and pour over a green salad. Garnish with slices of radish or parsley leaves.

Drying Fruit for the Winter

Core and slice apples and pears. Cut plums and apricots in half, removing the stones.

Put parchment/greaseproof baking paper on baking sheets; spread out the fruit slices in a single layer and let them dry slowly at F110–130°/40–50°C in the oven or on a radiator. The fruit could also be cut into small pieces, strung on strong thread or twine and hung up to dry. Apple peel can be dried for tea.

▲ *Children like to build their own "apple ladders." Several dowels can be joined together with string; knots in the string keep the rungs separated.*

◄ *Making dried apples: Peel and core the apples. Cut thin slices and hang on an apple drying stand. Dry them in a warm, dry place and then put the pieces in a jar for a winter treat.*

Oats, Peas, Beans and Barley Grow

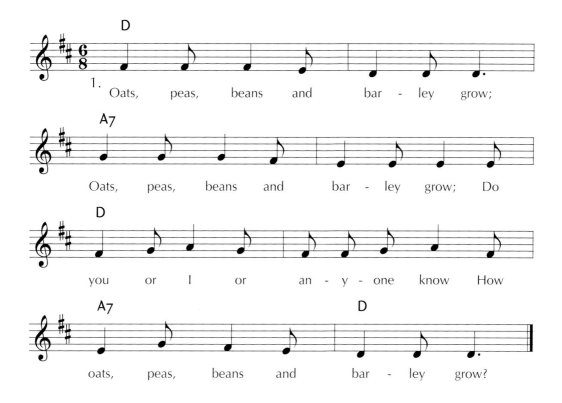

1. Oats, peas, beans and bar-ley grow;
Oats, peas, beans and bar-ley grow; Do
you or I or an-y-one know How
oats, peas, beans and bar-ley grow?

2. First the farmer sows his seed,
   Then he stands and takes his ease:
   (fold arms)
   Stamps his foot and claps his hand,
   And turns around to view the land.
   (shade eyes)

3. Waiting for a partner,
   Waiting for a partner,
   Open the ring and take one in,
   And then we'll happily dance and sing.

Haying Circle Play

Polish folk song

1. On a Mon - day morn - ing, sun - ny Mon - day morn - ing, Sowed our seed, Ta - tus* and I, Sowed it when the sun was high, Sowed our seed, Ta - tus and I, Sowed it when the sun was high.

* pronounced Ta-toosh — Polish for "father"

2. On a Tuesday morning, sunny Tuesday morning,
   Mowed our hay, Tatus and I,
   Mowed it when the sun was high ...
   (large, rhythmical cutting of the scythe)

3. On a Wednesday morning ...
   Dried our hay, Tatus and I ...
   (bend from waist, reach down to gather hay, then toss it high)

4. On a Thursday morning ...
   Raked our hay, Tatus and I ...
   (large, rhythmical raking gesture)

5. On a Friday morning ...
   Hauled our hay, Tatus and I ...
   (scoop up hay in arms, then drop it into "wagon")

6. On a Saturday morning ...
   Sold our hay, Tatus and I
   (offer hay in outstretched arms)

7. On a Sunday morning ...
   Bowed our heads, Tatus and I,
   Thanked the Lord who dwells on high ...
   (bow heads, fold hands or cross arms in gratitude)

The following Norse fairy tale is a good story to tell at this time of year.

The little pot that was always full

There was once a little house. It was pitiful looking, standing askew and about to fall down. In it lived a young woman. She had spent her last penny and used up all her food. She had only a little pot and that was empty.

The young woman washed the little pot clean and rinsed it out, and placed it in front of the door to dry in the sun. Suddenly, the little pot started to run away!

It jumped down the steps and ran pell-mell down the street.

What was it doing, this freshly washed and rinsed little pot? Well, I will tell you. It ran to the butcher's shop, and there the butcher's helper, a young man, was cutting up meat for soup. It ran there, and then it came back. But look, the pot was no longer empty. Something was in it.

Next it climbed up the steps and knocked at the door.

The young woman heard the knocking and called, "Who is there?"

"Little Full-Pot"

"Little pot, what have you brought with you?"

"Look in my big belly."

"Soup-meat and fat. Who gave it to you?"

"The table was too small and it fell in."

"Oh, you good little pot. Come in and we will cook it."

And the young woman immediately took the soup-meat and began to cook it so that it sizzled, and the little house began to dance with joy. The thick, pleasing aroma rose up the chimney.

On another morning, the young woman had again washed and rinsed the little pot and put it on the steps to dry. And what do you think, the little pot again began to run. It leaped down the steps and ran pell-mell down the street.

Do you know where it ran this time? It ran to the baker's. Just then, the baker's boy was shaking the fresh-baked biscuits out onto the table. The pot ran in.

Wait a moment. It will soon come back. There it is already. And again it has brought something back.

"Who's there?"

"Little Full-Pot."

"Little pot, what have you brought?"

"Look in my big belly!"

"The whole pot is full. Who gave them to you?"

"The table was too small and they fell in."

"Oh, good little pot, come in and we will eat."

The young woman took the honey biscuits out of the pot, brewed sweet coffee and drank and ate so happily that the little house again began to dance for joy, and the delicious aromas poured out of the chimney.

This really pleased the poor young woman.

On the next day, very early she had already nicely washed and rinsed the little pot and had put it out to dry on the steps. And again it began to run. It sprang down the steps and ran along the street. And where was the little pot running? I know. To the tavern. There the peasants were sitting and paying their coins.

And not long afterward, it came back again, bump, bump, bump against the door.

"Who's there?"

"Little Full-Pot."

"Little pot, what have you brought with you?"

"Look in my big belly!"

"Real gold coins! Who gave them to you?"

"The table was too small and they fell in."

Oh, good little pot, come right in and we will count the money."

The young woman immediately took the pot and shook out all the coins and turned them over and over so that the little house again danced for joy, and the last bit of smoke went out the chimney.

Now you can imagine how happy the young woman was. But she wanted more. And becoming quite greedy, she thought: Why should I wait until tomorrow morning to send the little pot? It can bring me something more today. So without washing or rinsing the little pot, she just put it out on the steps.

And indeed the little pot began to run. It leaped down the steps and ran down the street until it came to the marketplace. And it stood there. The market had ended and the little mice had collected what was left over.

Now a little mouse slipped into the little pot to take a nap. As the little pot noticed that, it went home very softly and quietly and knocked on the door.

"Who's outside?"

"Little Full-Pot"

"Oh, good little pot, come in quickly." What do you have this time, thought the young woman as she reached curiously into the pot. And out sprang the mouse.

"Oh you bad little pot, you," cried the young woman and became so angry that she threw the little pot out the door. And the little pot broke in pieces.

When the young woman came out of the house and saw that the little pot was broken, she began to cry and said, "I am a poor young woman, what shall I do now?"

Fortunately, a farmer came along the way and said, "Come to my farm and you can milk the cows."

So the young woman went with the farmer to his farm and milked the cows, and was satisfied.

OCTOBER

Basket-making

House-building

Before the withering leaves die and fall, bushes and trees are radiant with yellow, orange, red and brown

the winter during his hibernation. The squirrels are filling their storehouses to the brim, and the dormouse is also doing what's necessary to survive the cold.

Green, the colour of the plant world's life forces, retreats during October. As light and warmth decrease, plants start to wither and take on other colours.

Nature is again enveloped in magical hues. October is the most colourful month of the second half of the year. Fields and forest are radiant in many shades as the light from the low lying sun shines upon them — at least until the first cold winds.

Autumn has come and taken away
the lovely summer dress
the fields have worn,
and has scattered the leaves.
As the stinging winter winds blow
the earth covers itself, warm and cosy,
with the colourful leaves, and they,
already quite tired, drift off to sleep.

Joseph von Eichendorff

As long as we are still in the sign of Libra (until October 21) and the days and nights are literally in balance, October is still golden and the fruit is ripening in the early autumn sun, becoming sweet and juicy. We can see and hear the hedgehog eating in the fruit garden. He is building up a protective layer of fat that will see him through

Children can work in the garden until the end of October. Nature is giving us her last gifts of the year. Now, seed-bearing grasses and hawthorn and ash twigs are gathered. These can be bundled and dried to have ready as food for the birds when there is snow and deep frost. This way, children learn about the foods that birds eat in the wild (see pages 63–66: Caring for birds).

Basket-making

At this time, take note of the bushes and trees that have lost their leaves; perennial flower bushes by the pond; and plants that have grown out of control on the walls of the house, pergolas and trellises. There will be lots here that can be used to make simple baskets, mats, trivets and other items.

Making baskets with plant materials gives a wonderful feeling of being connected with the natural world. Archaeological research indicates that basketry is one of the oldest types of handicraft. In all earlier cultures, human beings used baskets to carry home grains, nuts, berries, herbs, wood and many other items that they harvested or collected.

Today, people still go on harvesting and gathering outings — but this takes place not in the woods, but in the supermarket. They receive items second- or third-hand, rather than doing the harvesting themselves. Instead of a willow basket, they put things in a steel shopping cart. The direction of this history speaks for itself.

Baskets and woven items serve various purposes:

* gathering, drying and storage
* furniture and clothing
* transportation
* boats and shelters

Nature has provided every region of the earth with plants that can be used in basketry. There are a great many such plants. Even today, people use the same methods for making baskets as were used in very ancient cultures.

A carrying basket used in Germany in earlier times

If children come along on the search for materials, they will learn about the shape, colour, form and structure of plants. The particular characteristics of different materials indicate the way they can be used. In gathering, one has to be careful not to pick any plants that are protected as rare or endangered types. If there is an abundant supply of one material, it can be used, but care should be taken that enough is left for the plants to grow luxuriantly again in the next growing season.

Plants Used for Basket-Making

* Climbing and creeping plants, *clematis, evergreens, honeysuckle, ivy:*

For these plants, October is the best time for harvesting. The young creepers are just beginning to turn woody and are still flexible. They already have a certain stability and strength. If

35

the material has a tendency to break, it should be soaked in warm water before use.

❀ Tree shoots, *maple, willow, ash, hazelnut, apple, plum and other fruit trees:*

The shoots that have grown over the summer provide strong and attractively coloured material for basketry. Mixing green and red shoots can produce especially beautiful effects.

❀ Grasses and grass-like plants, *wheat, rye, oats, barley, corn/maize, sea grass, rushes, reeds, iris, sword lily:*

Cereal grain stalks should be harvested during the grain harvest, that is, at the end of July. They can be used immediately, but you must allow for substantial drying and shrinkage that will make the basket quite loose. Alternatively, you can store and dry the stalks. To make them flexible again, soak them for two hours in lukewarm water.

Grass, lily leaves, corn/maize and rushes need to be worked when newly harvested.

❀ Roots: Tree roots are best collected in an area where a storm has blown down trees. For older children, a visit with adults to such a place can be an unforgettable experience.

❀ Bark, *maple, lime, willow, white birch, cherry, hemlock, pine:*

When a tree has been cut down, strip pieces of bark that are as long as possible using a draw-knife or spokeshave. The bark can be used when it is quite fresh. The best bark is from young trees. The best time of year for harvesting bark is in the early spring when the sap has begun to flow but before the shoots have begun to appear.

Making a Willow Basket or a Hanging Basket for Flowers

Newly-cut willow shoots must be soaked in water for two or three weeks before use.

You will need the following tools:

❀ a sturdy knife
❀ a small pair of pliers or tweezers
❀ a basketry awl for making space to insert a new shoot.

Begin the willow basket with a cross base, a star base, or a rectangular base. (See illustrations opposite.) When the bottom is finished, bend the shoots 90 degrees and weave the sides of the basket. For finishing off the lip of the basket, cut the shoots, moisten them again, then bend and weave them back into the basket. The following sketches show several basic techniques.

Basket base and the beginning of the side. The spokes of young privet shoots are interwoven with wild grape tendrils.

Japanese-style base
(cross base)

Star base

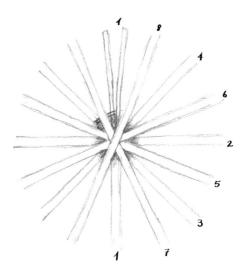

1. Laying the base of spokes

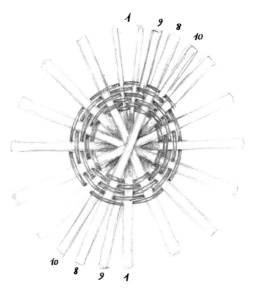

2. Fixing the spokes in place by weaving

Rectangular base

Finishing the lip of the basket

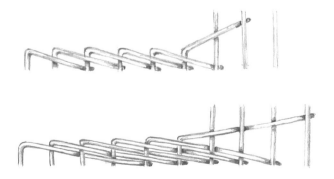

A flower basket is an ideal basketry project, even in kindergarten

With a little help, even four-year-olds can weave a flower basket. In the photo above, shoots of a privet hedge are used as the spokes for a frame and wild grape creepers are woven through them. The bottom is laid out as a star base; it then develops a rounded ball form, and finally comes to a point.

Because the base and the sides are not woven separately, this is an excellent project for children.

To make the lip of the basket very stable, it is important to soak the material so that it doesn't crack when bent

Weaving Round or Oval Objects

When we want to weave a round or oval object — a place mat, pan holder, beehive or house slippers — we need long material such as slender twigs or shoots that can be built up in layers. These are best worked when fresh. The new shoots of the plum tree, maple, lime and hazelnut serve very well. They are sewn together using a blunt needle and heavy craft thread. This work is appropriate for children from the first grade (6-7-years-old) on.

▲ *Begin with a switch: start the oval pattern with very young willow switches that have not become woody yet; with reeds; with very long, new straw; or other hard grasses. Bend one strand of the material into the desired form, then lay another strand on top and attach it with the "Indian stitch" or the (somewhat more difficult) "simple stitch."*

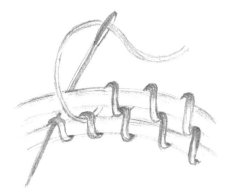

Simple stitch: the "simple stitch" is more difficult but can be used instead of the "Indian stitch." Very dexterous children can use it as a supplemental technique.

Place mats made from wood can be finished with a woven edge. Drill holes in the plywood, pull the plaiting material through them, and then weave around the edge.

Older children can make beautiful toys or practical items such as a miniature baby carriage. For the bottom you will need a piece of thin plywood, to which the poles are attached. Two axles with two wheels each are attached to the bottom. The sides and tops are woven of some fine material. Finally the handle of the carriage is inserted.

◀ *Indian stitch: while this stitch is relatively easy to master, it requires much patience since the stitches are very close to each other. It results in a very stable piece of work.*

Mashenka and the bear

A Russian tale

There was once a grandmother and grandfather, and they lived in a hut on the edge of the forest. They had a granddaughter named Mashenka. One day, Mashenka wanted to go into forest and said:

"Dear grandfather and grandmother, I don't want to stay inside any longer. I want to go into the woods and gather mushrooms and berries. Oh, please let me go."

The two old people answered:

"Yes, go right away, sweet child, and pick the little berries quickly, and also the mushrooms that grow on short stems and on long stalks. Just be careful on the way, and come home before it is dark."

Mashenka went into the forest. She picked berries and mushrooms and, finding more and more, went deeper and deeper into the forest. But she lost her way. She ran and ran and finally came to a hut made of rough, unhewn logs. She knocked and said:

"Please let me in, please let me in. Who lives in this hut; who lives in this lonely hut? Is there nobody at home?"

There was no answer, so she went in and waited. In the hut lived a bear. When he came home in the evening and saw the little girl, he growled:

"GRRROWL, GRRROWL, who is sitting there? I will never let you go away. You will tend my stove and cook my gruel and bring me my food."

So Mashenka had to stay with the bear and serve him, cook for him and bake for him. And when he went out into the woods for the day, he said to her:

"You must stay in the house. You must stay in the house and not take a single step outside. If I find you in the forest, I will surely eat you up!"

Mashenka had such a deep longing to see her grandmother and grandfather that she thought and thought about what she could do to get home again. She took flour and milk and made a beautiful, delicious cake and said to the bear:

"Oh, brown bear, I ask of you, please let me go back to my village, just for one day. I would like to bring this cake to my grandmother and grandfather."

But he didn't want to let her go. He said:

"GRRRRROWL, GRRRRRROWL, that cannot be. Give me that sweet, lovely cake and I will bring it to the village myself. But you will stay here at home."

That was just what Mashenka wanted. She fetched the large carrying basket and said to the bear:

"Now look at this sweet, delicious cake. I am putting it in the basket and you will carry it to the village and take it to my grandfather and grandmother. But do not nibble on my cake, and do not lift the cloth that covers it. I will climb the oak tree and be watching you. Go outside now and see what the weather is like."

The bear was satisfied and went out to see if it was raining or snowing. Mashenka jumped into the basket with the cake and pulled the cloth over herself. When the bear came back, Mashenka was not to be seen. But the basket was there, and he put it on his arm and set out on his journey.

He walked and walked. The cake smelled so sweet! So he sat down on a tree stump to rest and said:

"I will sit on this stump and have a bit of cake."

Then Mashenka called from the basket:

"I see you, I see you.

"Do not sit on the tree stump and do not eat the cake!

"Take it to my dear grandmother and grandfather."

He picked up the basket again and walked on. After he had gone quite a way and the sweet aroma of the cake wafted up to his nose, he decided to try again and again sat down.

"I will sit down on this tree stump and have a bit of cake."

But again Mashenka called out from the basket:

"I see you! I see you! Don't sit on the tree stump and don't eat my cake. Take it to my dear grandmother and dear grandfather."

The bear was surprised:

"She's watching me, she's watching me. Yes, she's clever and sees everything quite clearly. She's on the very top of the oak tree."

With a sigh he took the basket again and went into the village. He knocked at the house of the grandfather.

"GRRRRROWL. Open quickly. I have brought something from Mashenka."

Then the dogs in the village began to bark: "WOOF WOOF WOOF."

The bear was frightened. He put the basket down and ran away as fast as his legs could carry him. Then the grandmother and grandfather came out of the house. There seemed to be a basket there. They said:

"What could be in this basket? Let us take a look inside. What have we here? A lovely cake and also our dear Mashenka, sweet and happy!"

How happy were the good old folks to have Mashenka healthy and safe with them again. And Mashenka also was full of joy.

House-building

Once the craft of basketry has been mastered, it can be used to make a shelter or little house. Everyone will want to be involved. It is a basic human need to build a place to live where one can find shelter from the heat and icy cold, from the rain and wind.

The first human beings — in the wild, unprotected and unarmed — needed a shelter for survival. With a shelter, you can raise children, store food and protect yourself from enemies. Equipped with a healthy human intelligence and two skilful hands, human beings all over the world build homes that are appropriate for the particular climate, geology and plant life of where they live. In Germany, for example, houses traditionally have been made of fieldstone, oaken beams, plaited willow and hazelnut branches held together with a plaster of mud, cow manure, straw and sand.

A typical style of exposed-beam building used in an area near Cologne

In many parts of Germany, people still build homes in the traditional style with the beams of the framework visible

Simple Houses and Huts

When building a shelter, people typically use the materials in their immediate environment. Walls may be made of animal skins and brushwood, woven plant materials, or of stone and mud. Wood is usually used for the roof and is covered with animal skins, straw, grass or bark.

The illustrations opposite provide several examples that can be constructed in miniature or built on a large scale outdoors. Regardless of which culture, time period or geographical area the various models come from, they serve as cultural-historical examples for the children. They give children a sense of the development of human shelter from the simplest "roof over one's head" to the modern skyscraper made of steel and concrete. Also, they stimulate the imagination to create beautiful scenes of human habitation in nature.

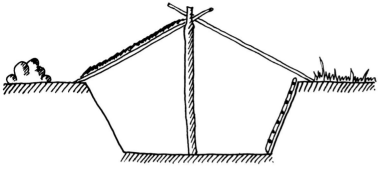

Trench house with a roof of animal skins over a wood frame. (To build the model, use fir or pine branches for the roof.)

Tent: pole frame covered with animal skins

Brushwood tent: built with sapling trunks, branches, grasses, moss, reeds and other such materials

Woven tent: made of strong wooden poles with flexible smaller branches woven in

Round stone house mortared with mud: the roof is made from a stone slab or a piece of wood

Building: Putting down Roots

In the course of history, cultures have had increasing contact with each other. Through these points of contact, architectural patterns have developed that are evident in different regions and different historical periods.

In early human dwellings, the wind could blow through the plaited walls and the sun, moon and stars shone into them. The natural senses of the people were similarly open, sensitive and permeable, and their lives were closely bound to nature. Since then, human beings have become increasingly isolated from nature.

Our present industrial society with its specialization of function has, for most people, taken away the experience of building one's own house. Most of us today live in apartments that are arranged next to and above or below one another, or in houses in large developments, and have very little chance to develop our personal vision of a home.

However, ideas such "finding oneself" and "finding one's home" are increasingly widespread.

Wattle and daub house: walls of woven wood plastered with mud, roof of logs covered with sod

House with gabled roof: wicker house with forked poles supporting a pointed roof

Circular hut: beam construction with a straw roof and walls made of clay "loaves"

Their prevalence suggests that we are searching for a situation in which we are sheltered — that there is a hunger to return to a wholeness which has been lost.

In education in the 1970s, there was a tendency to turn away from nature. Since then, there has been a total rethinking: treeless playgrounds covered with asphalt are being broken up and replanted, and inhuman school buildings and environments cut off from nature are being transformed. (See the description of building an arbor on pages 46 and 47.)

Building a willow arbor in a park in a small city in Germany is an intercultural and intergenerational project

◄ *Tying willow branches into a bundle ...*

▲ *forming the arch ...*

▲ *enjoying the space*

▼ *A plaited willow fence is a protective barrier at the edge of a steep slope*

Building an arbor in a partially paved schoolyard

◄ Deep holes must be dug into the earth

▲ Sturdy bundles of willow branches are tied together ...

▲ and wait to be used

▼ Little bundles of branches are used for stabilization

◄ *Many hands are necessary to carry the willow bundles to the site*

► *The construction is already taking shape*

▲ *Many hands make the work go fast*

▼ *The "roof star" came out especially well*

Today, social and financial factors mean that living conditions for children are becoming increasingly crowded. Schools are also too crowded. There is an acute shortage of space as the number of children grows and rooms exceed their capacity. Children simply do not have enough room, and this manifests in aggressive behaviour and brutality in all areas of life.

Also, because there is less and less physical activity, the feeling of being dislocated increases. One does not experience one's own body. One does not feel at home in oneself. Always being "in" but never "at home" can lead to restlessness, anxiety and vandalism. The traditional "making oneself a home" for the sake of being protected has given way to self-centredness in a world where value has been lost. What is actual reality and what is merely another's delusions? In the vast confusion of modern media-based life, it is hard to distinguish what is real from what is not, particularly for children and young people.

Nowadays in our kindergartens and schools we have many students from other countries who feel disoriented and homeless. They have been robbed of their native tongue and fall silent about their hopelessness and vulnerability. It is important to

Building as an Archetypal Experience

The architect and builder Marcel Kalberer, who specializes in natural building, describes building as an archetypal experience:

Experience: I have many unforgettable memories of huts of leaves and of snow, of joy in the building and sadness in the destruction, and I have observed countless building projects carried out by children and young people. I am certain that the experience of building shelters plays an indispensable role in the development of personality.

Realization: In his or her first building project — be it an igloo, or hut made of mud or twigs — the child takes a big step in becoming a person, in creating a space in which to be, and for the first time creating personal protection and shelter.

bring them into contact with nature in an active and wholesome way. Taking up crafts and outdoor activity can make some small contribution to the creation of a relationship between humanity and nature.

Imaginative Structures: Large and Small

We must reacquaint the younger generation with first-hand, practical experiences such as building your own house — even if the house is very small. Otherwise, their experiences of life will be all second- or third-hand.

To start things off, you can discuss different questions with the children. What makes a home cosy? What does comfort mean? How can a warm environment, neither too warm nor too cold, be achieved efficiently? What, in fact, is beauty? And so on. These concepts are brought to life and given meaning by working with your hands with real things.

The clothing worn by the builders shows them to be people of today. Otherwise you could think this hut belonged to a much earlier period of history. It was built during holiday time as a family project.

During the same holiday, this tower was built by a father and son. The work was challenging and they enjoyed working together.

Perception: In an age when we are increasingly estranged from nature, we need to find our way back to the natural and cultural roots of our existence. While the artificial and virtual world dulls the senses, the playful work of building something with natural materials offers the senses and the spirit many different perceptual possibilities.

Thought: Even building the smallest leaf hut awakens the imagination and the spirit of invention in the builder. Also it involves artistic and engineering decisions, requires organizational and technical considerations in relation to materials and tools, and strengthens the readiness to work cooperatively, helping one another. And, of course, it is a playful, joyful activity.

Touching and Understanding: Building with snow, mud, branches and twigs, stamping and kneading, bending and breaking with hands and feet: these are all experiences of the sense of touch, and as such, they help the human spirit to be recognized and experienced.

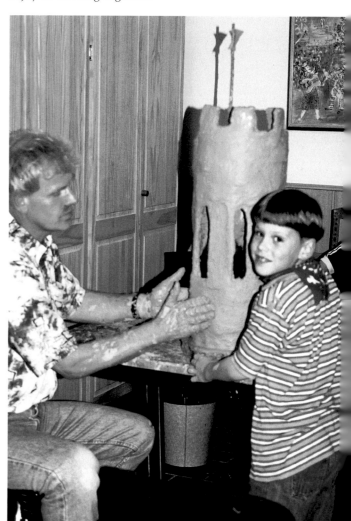

Memory: Watching them work with branches, twigs, shoots, grasses and the mixture of mud and straw, I always think what a wonderful thing it is that children, with very little help from adults, know how to make imaginative and sturdy buildings. Unselfconsciously and drawing on their own intuition, they replicate the history of building in our civilization.

House-building is especially well suited to cooperative projects involving young and old. Parents can participate at weekends or during holidays. Young children cannot really manage some of the work without the help of adults.

With all house and hut models, it is important that there is a sturdy but transportable base. Stone tiles are good for constructions using mud and stone. Pieces of wood or board are helpful when a wooden construction requires drilled holes for stability.

The natural materials for the huts — mud and clay, forked branches, round pieces of wood and material for plaiting and weaving — should, if possible, be carefully collected from the immediate environment.

As these imaginative structures took shape, all the workers, young and old, developed imagination and manual skills through intense working, alone and together. There was a lively sharing and exchange of skills.

Building a House Together: Developing Social Skills

In the various structures shown here, the builder found the material in the immediate environment. It is obvious that in each case the chosen material influenced the character of the structure.

The house-building project is excellent for teacher-training students. The pictures opposite show work that was done by students in the Dortmund Waldorf teacher training. Besides having educational value, the project allowed the thirty-two participants, coming from various nations and thrown together for two weeks, to form a social community.

The structures are very varied. They demonstrate the imagination and joy with which these young citizens of the world will be able to bring a fresh intercultural impulse into their teaching. The aim of the project was achieved: to understand oneself through cooperative handicraft activities.

Pictures on the right — clockwise from top left:

Rapunzel's Tower: architectural elements from different cultures (German, Argentinian and Nepalese) overcame language and intercultural barriers.

House of the Red Sun: in this structure the Japanese influence is very clear.

The Ikebana arbor

The woman who built this crèche maintained that she was not at all artistic or creative and that she wouldn't be able to make the figures for the crèche. But since every human being is an artist, she did in fact create something that is truly beautiful. The work gave her courage and convinced her that she could be creative.

A sturdy prison, an airy tree house, and a cosy stall for animals all were made during this time

▲▼ *The House of the Seven Souls: Seven young men and women worked together to build a house of wood and mud plaster. First the house had a slanted roof which was later replaced with a gabled roof.*

▲ *Festival of the flower children: This little Arab girl used beech twigs for a north African mud construction.*

◄ *A solid but inviting castle made of stones and mud*

House-Building in the Third Grade

The house models shown in the pictures below were built by groups of third grade (9–10-years-old) students in the Waldorf school in Gummersbach, Germany, as part of their handicraft class. All the materials — even the pieces of tree trunk that serve as bases for the structures — were gathered from the immediate environment.

The wealth of ideas and the dexterity of children in the third and fourth grades is such that they scarcely need to be given instructions. Simply offer a little help, now and then; for example, the teacher should drill the holes into the wooden slabs.

A fortress with drawbridge

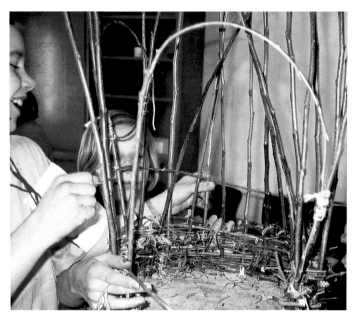

The frame of this construction was made of shoots from an apple tree which were formed into a pointed tent. Broom grass was woven through the supports to make the walls.

A frame of wooden poles was anchored in holes drilled into a piece of tree trunk, and the walls were built of many tiny mud bricks. The top of an old Christmas tree covered with bundles of grass served as the roof.

The Carpenters

Puerto Rican folk song

With vigour

3. O see the masons working,
   mixing the mortar;
   we love to watch them working,
   mixing the mortar.
   They go *swish,* we go *swoosh,*
   they go *swish,* we go *swoosh,*
   until we've mixed the mortar,
   Finished at last!

4. O see the masons working,
   putting the bricks in;
   we love to watch them working,
   putting the bricks in.
   They go *clink,* we go *clank,*
   they go *clink,* we go *clank,*
   until we've put the bricks in.
   Finished at last!

From *Sing Through the Day* reproduced by permission of The Plough Publishing House

A Dedication Ceremony

At the end of the house-building — whether it
involves children or adults — there is a dedication
ceremony with an appropriate verse.

May the light of your soul guide you.
May the light of your soul bless the work that you do
with the secret love and warmth of your heart.
May you see in what you do the beauty of your own soul.

John O'Donoghue

Bless the four corners of this house,
   And be the lintel blessed,
And bless the hearth and bless the board,
   And bless each place of rest.

And bless the door which opens wide,
   To strangers as to kin,
And bless each crystal window pane
   That lets the sunshine in;

And bless the rooftree overhead,
   And every sturdy wall —
The peace of man, the peace of God,
   The peace of love on all.

Traditional

Fruit in a blossom,
And petals in a seed,
Reeds in a river bed,
And music in a reed:
Stars in a firmament
Shining in the night,
Sun in a galaxy,
And planet in its light;
Bones in the rosy blood
Like land in the sea.
Marrow in a skeleton,
And I in me.

Owen Barfield

May the blessed sunlight
shine upon you and warm your heart till it glows
like a great peat fire, so that the stranger may
come and warm himself at it, as well as the friend.
And may the light shine out of the eyes of you,
like a candle set in the windows of a house,
bidding the wanderer to come in out of the storm.

Traditional

NOVEMBER

Caring for birds

Working with beeswax

In November, the world of nature, after the luxuriant growth and varied activities of summer, settles down for a rest. The hedgehog and the other hibernating animals look for warm quarters. The geese, who at the autumnal equinox were in the far north, now fly south in a V-formation, saying farewell with their loud honking.

The light of the sun becomes ever weaker. Nature seems dull and colourless, and the final leaves are falling. A shadow of transience gradually spreads across the landscape and calls forth a dark, death-like feeling.

In the roots and seeds of the plant world, life sleeps through the winter, yearning for the liberating sunshine of the spring while enveloped in cold fog, frost and snow.

The scorpion is truly an appropriate symbol of this time of year. It lives in the earth, shies away from the light and often greets its fellow creatures with the threatening gesture of its erect, deadly tail. The upward pointing arrow in the symbol for the zodiacal sign of Scorpio (♏) means that, in spite of death, there is always hope for new life.

> One generation passes away,
>   and another generation comes:
> But the earth abides for ever.
> The sun also rises, and the sun goes down,
> And hastens to his place where he arose.
>
> The wind goes towards the south,
> And turns about unto the north;
> It whirls about continually,
> And the wind returns again
>   according to his circuits.
>
> All the rivers run into the sea;
> Yet the sea is not full:
> Unto the place whence the rivers come,
> There they return again.

from Ecclesiastes

North Wind

The north wind doth blow and we shall have snow And what will poor rob-in do then, poor thing? He'll sit in the barn and keep him-self warm And hide his head un-der his wing, poor thing.

Caring for birds

With the end of the growing season, the work in the garden also comes to a temporary halt. This is an opportunity to look back upon the rich bounty that nature gives us every year. It is also a chance to think about the time of dying off and about the winter rest of the earth.

In order to receive nature's future gifts, a certain foresight is necessary. In recent times, the self-restorative powers of nature have become weakened because of people's thoughtless and selfish behavior. The need for loving and healing intervention must become obvious and universally accepted.

We should not destroy what we love. In looking back gratefully, in thinking critically about the here and now, and in considering the future, we should ask ourselves: do our actions adequately express our love of nature, to be an example for our children?

We should seek assistance for this very important task. Help can be found through many organizations dedicated to protecting the natural environment.

With this in mind, what can we do at this time of year? In the surroundings of every kindergarten — even if it is in a city — are several varieties of native birds. Particularly in urban areas, it is important to pay special attention to them. With very little expense and a lot of persistence, we can support and protect them in a way that is relevant to children. The ornithologist and naturalist Joachim Hecht has written the following on this theme:

What we can do to protect birds

We human beings are constantly reducing the habitat of the animal world. For the most part, we do so unconsciously. Nevertheless, there are a great many human activities that lead to the reduction and even the destruction of natural habitats. There are fewer and fewer hedges between fields, and because the number of fields, meadows and farms is constantly decreasing, birds' food supply is also decreasing.

That should be reason enough to think seriously about how we can change things. I will concern myself here only with the birds in our immediate environment.

Birds look for places to feed, breed and nest in human residential areas. Human beings also need green spaces in cities, and gardens. These areas can offer birds a bountiful food supply, especially when there is a surrounding hedge for protection.

Such green areas can include bushes that produce berries such as rosehip, sloe and elderberry. Here birds can find insects, seeds from trees and grasses, worms and many other kinds of food.

Trees and hedges provide nesting places, but it's important to differentiate between birds that nest in holes, and those that nest in the open. Finches make their nests in the open, in trees, bushes and hedges. The blackbird, with its beautiful song, does as well.

Most varieties of titmouse — who are especially beloved and useful since they eat harmful insects — nest in holes. For them we must provide nesting places by hanging up nesting boxes in trees. Also, don't forget the starlings and the nuthatches: they need nesting boxes with larger holes. Wherever possible, one should orient the boxes so that the opening looks toward the rising sun.

In order to raise their young and to sing, birds need quiet places. In autumn, the nesting boxes must be cleaned out to get rid of old nesting material and vermin. Sweep out all corners and cracks with a brush. This way, we can give the birds a clean, safe shelter for the cold winter. When cleaning out the nesting boxes you often find mouse, bee and wasp nests.

Whenever and wherever possible, human beings must consider their fellow creatures, and protect their living space from noise and visual intrusion. More information about birds, including instructions for building a nesting box can be found in *Spring* in this book series.

Food for Birds

Winter has begun. Every year we ask: how can we help the birds survive the harsh conditions? A bird table by a window is usually possible. Children can spread grass seeds they have gathered in the summer on it, or plantain, or a commercial bird-seed mix. All birds love oat flakes. Even an apple that has begun to go bad can be put out.

It is helpful to keep a patch of grass in the yard free of snow, and also to put out water for the birds. For this, you'll need a flat, frost-proof plate that you fill once or several times a day with warm water during periods of sub-freezing temperature. Of course, this drinking dish must be kept clean.

In the cold of winter we should give the birds fat. You can buy balls of fat or suet wrapped in a wire mesh that can be hung in a tree. Birds also like scrap fat from the butcher's shop. Put a handful-sized piece in a nylon mesh bag (the kind oranges and other fruit are often sold in) and hang it in a tree.

Making your own bird food

Natural winter food for the birds should be gathered in late summer and autumn, and thoroughly dried.

Along paths we can find stalks of grains and seed-bearing grasses, including stinging nettle, yarrow, St John's wort and white ox-eye.

From the edge of the forest, gather seeds from the black and red elderberry, sloe, rosehip and

During the winter it is important to keep areas of grass free of snow so that the birds who feed on the ground can find something to eat

hawthorn, and seed cones from pine, larch, spruce and fir.

If you want to make birdfeed from this, make a fire in an appropriate fireplace (see *Summer* in this book series). Then take solidified vegetable fat (6–10 pounds, 3–5 kg) of vegetable margarine or coconut fat), melt it in a large pot, and mix in the dried seeds that we have gathered from the garden, fields, meadows and forest until all are covered with the fat. Then, let the mixture cook briefly at a high temperature. This prevents mould from forming later on.

The next step is to put the mixture into clay flower pots. While it is cooling in the cooking pot, attach branches to flower pots to serve as perches for the birds. Attach the branches with string and then make a loop for hanging the feeder on a tree. (See the photos on page 66.)

Finally, fill the flower pots with the mixture, compact it well, and let the pot stand until the bird food mixture is hardened. Start feeding the birds when ice and snow have arrived, limiting their access to food.

This is a good method of making bird food using seeds that the birds would find in their environment. In a clay flower pot equipped with perches, the feed stays clean.

66

Working with beeswax

Modelling with Beeswax

At this cold time of year it is a real blessing for the children to be able to do modelling with the warm, aromatic beeswax. Give them enough wax so that they can work with both hands and have enough to make a little house.

For a kindergarten group of 25 children, you need at least 9 pounds (4 kg) of beeswax.

➤ *Prepare the beeswax according to the following recipe:*

Put 2 pounds (1 kg) of pure beeswax in an enamelled pan (preferably a flat one), place in an oven heated to F150°/70°C, and let it melt. Stir in well 2 ounces (60 g) of lanolin (*adeps lanae*, available from a pharmacy/chemist shop). Let the mixture slowly cool until it is hard. Remove the hardened wax with a wooden spoon and place on wax/greaseproof paper. Then break the wax into wax "dumplings" that are the right size for the hands of the children. Put these back into the flat pot. Wax prepared in this way can be remelted many times.

An hour to an hour and a half before the modelling session, warm the wax in the oven at F125°/50°C — being careful that it doesn't melt.

The children's creations are transformed again and again into something new. You can place the modeled piece back into the pot, warm the wax and roll it into a new ball that the children can work with again.

A wooden board or a cross-section of a tree trunk are good work surfaces.

The beeswax mixed with lanolin stays malleable for 15 to 30 minutes, then becomes hard and stable. Many little works of art can be made from beeswax. This wonderfully aromatic, precious material appeals to the children's impulse to give something form and to experience the joy of creation.

Beeswax: A Precious Material

After the modelling session, all the wax can be carefully collected, even the tiniest crumb, so that none of the precious material is lost.

While the children are working with the wax, we can tell them stories about bees, such as those in Jakob Streit's *Animal Stories*. This will help them to understand how precious the honey and the wax are that the bees have laboured long and hard to make during the summer, gathering pollen from the colourful flowers and carrying it back to their hives (see *Spring* in this book series).

◄ *A sage bush in full bloom in the garden of the Children's Nature and Garden Centre*

Looking into the honey centrifuge

◄◄ *A little boy holds a hive frame with bees still on it. The bees have filled out the frame with wax honeycombs for breeding and for storing food. Now in winter the wax can be used for modelling.*

▼ *A solar wax melter with many pieces of honeycomb*

◄ *... and what is this? The retinue of the queen bee? Almost! The warmth of the sun has transformed the pieces of wax in the solar melter into a sweet-smelling array of fairy-tale figurines. The children can see how the golden wax for modeling and for making candles is obtained.*

Even better than the stories is the experience, in summer, of helping adults create a perfect environment for the bees — one filled with a variety of plants. In the Children's Nature and Garden Centre, we make sure that there is a variety of healing plants. That way, the bees have a sound diet that they can transform into beeswax and aromatic, delicious honey with powerful healing properties.

When the honeycombs are removed from the hive, they are placed in a honey centrifuge and

69

spun to extract the honey. The honey flows like liquid gold to the bottom of the centrifuge and through several fine sieves. A rich, delicious odour fills the room. What remains is the precious wax; the wax combs are gathered and put in the melter. Impurities are caught in the sieve as the wax runs down into the collecting tray.

Before the children's eyes, a process involving human beings and nature comes to its conclusion.

Spinning the honeycombs in the centrifuge

Dipping Candles

Making candles out of pure beeswax is a peaceful and enjoyable activity in the Advent season. A burning candle in this dark, cold time of the year is an outward sign of an inner light, a warmth to be conjured up in the dark days of November and during Advent. Candle-making is also an opportunity to involve children in the careful creation of gifts with real value.

Throughout the whole year, you can save the remnants of beeswax candles, making sure that they are of good quality and have no impurities in them. During Advent, these remnants of the past year can, with patient work, be made into new candles — a Christmas gift that brings warmth, love and joy and that can help create a true Christmas spirit within the family.

Instruction:
For one candle about 5 inches (12 cm) long and half an inch (1.5 cm) in diameter (the size of a Christmas tree candle), we need about 2/3 of an ounce (20 g) of beeswax and about 7 inches (18 cm) of sturdy wick cord. This can be obtained from a beekeeper, hobby store or bee-products specialty shop.

For the dipping process, you need twice as much wax as will go into the candles. Thus, if we want to make 25 to 30 candles with a group of children, we need 3 to 4 pounds (1.5–2 kg) of beeswax. If there aren't enough wax remnants, you can use fresh wax cut into small pieces for easy melting.

Important: the dipping pot should not be filled too full with cold wax because the wax expands when it is melted. It is better to add more later.

The children carefully and lovingly wrap the candles they have made. They have created these Christmas gifts with patience and joy.

The wax is melted in an enamelled metal container, in a water bath

The melting should proceed slowly, first over a very low heat that is slowly increased. It is very important that the pot for the hot water is almost as tall as the container holding the wax.

Put the container in the water pot and fill the pot until the water almost comes up to the lip of the container. It takes about an hour and a half for wax to melt in a water bath.

Caution: the wax at the bottom of the container will melt and want to expand, while the top layer is still hard, hindering the boiling. Therefore, under no circumstances should the top layer be pressed down. There is a danger that the hot bottom wax will shoot up and out like a geyser! This is a fire hazard!

For uniform melting, place two or three pieces of bent wire into the wax-container (see illustration). Something made from a metal that conducts heat, such as a piece of steel pipe, will also serve. This will allow the already melted wax at the bottom that needs to expand to rise to the top. The metal objects can be removed when all the wax has begun to melt.

Caution: never try to melt the wax in a pot directly on the burner without the water bath. This creates a serious fire hazard.

In candle-dipping, it is extremely important to maintain discipline and order among the children to prevent them from being injured by the hot, molten wax.

Children can manage candle-dipping best after they have been out playing in the fresh cold air. They'll be happy to be inside in the warm room and will be able to control their limbs. The candle-dipping can then be a harmonizing experience.

A holder for candles made from the upper trunk and branches of a small tree

Instead of a table, a long bench can be used for dipping. This helps maintain a fixed order as the children walk slowly around the bench. As they walk, they can sing songs about autumn, winter and Advent.

If the children don't have enough patience to finish their candles during one dipping session, the work can spread out over several days. This has the advantage that the unfinished candles can harden and cool and will "grow" more quickly and easily when they are dipped again (this is because the melted wax adheres better to an underlayer of cold, hardened wax).

When the wax is melted, the pot with the water bath, with the wax-container in it, is placed on a hot plate in the middle of the circle or on a table. One by one the children dip a candle in the melted wax, holding it by a loop in the wick at the top, and then letting the wax drip off and cool.

After five to seven dippings, the growing candle should be allowed to harden thoroughly. The best thing is to hang them on a stand made from the top of a small tree or to string them on a wooden pole and to take them outside for a time.

Meanwhile the water bath and the wax are both kept warm on the stove. More wax can be added if necessary. As the work continues, the children will be surprised at how quickly the cooled candles will grow.

After about fifteen dippings, the candles should already have become thick enough to use and you can decide whether or not they should be grown more. If they are thick enough, they can be shortened by cutting off about half an inch from the bottom where there is no wick.

Don't forget: when the work is finished, refill the wax-container and put the metal heat-transmitters in the still molten wax.

It is a very special experience for the children to do candle-dipping outside, with the wax melted in a pot over a campfire. In the clear, cold air of early winter, perhaps in the twilight, the contrast between the darkness and cold of the season and the warmth and light that emanates from the beeswax is especially strong. The aroma of the melted wax is balm for the respiratory system.

Dip by dip, layer by layer, the new candle comes into being. When dipping candles in the outdoors, the children strongly feel the contrast between the dark and cold of a November evening and the warm, aromatic beeswax which is a gift of summer.

Related Activities

* colouring candles
* pouring moulded candles
* rolling candles out of pressed sheets of beeswax
* looking at a honeycomb. It is amazing to see how the industrious bees have built storage rooms for the honey with great artistry and order. You can really appreciate the true worth of the beeswax.

The finished candles can be dipped in coloured wax

Candle-dipping

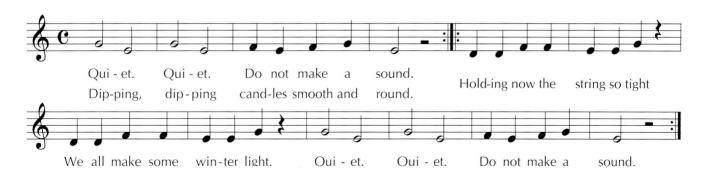

Qui - et.   Qui - et.   Do not make   a   sound.
Dip-ping,   dip - ping   cand-les smooth and   round.

Hold-ing now the   string so tight

We all make some   win-ter light.   Oui - et.   Oui - et.   Do not make   a   sound.

NOVEMBER

Making paper

Painting and handicrafts

Making paper

With the end of the growing season in November and the coming of the winter, paper-making is another excellent activity for children. During this time, plants are dying and the dead plants, made fibrous by the sun, rain, wind and the first frost, are available for use. Most of the organic substances in the plants have disintegrated and what remains is primarily the cellulose that gives the plant its structure. Cellulose fibers from grasses, ferns, stinging nettles and the leaves of local trees can be used in paper-making.

In our basket-making and house-building activities in October, we were concerned with the elasticity and stability of the plant materials. Now in November, we use the ongoing processes of decomposition to help us work with the parts of the plants that contain cellulose. We need only harvest them; there is no difficult preparation which uses water or energy.

Paper comes in many forms: as painting paper, writing paper, as the carrier of information in computer work, as books and packaging, as toilet paper and so on. We use paper every day in various forms, and we are largely unaware of the ecological cost of its production.

To convey to children an appreciation of the real value of paper, we will start with a collection of paper and show them how they can make their own paper using recycled paper with added plant matter and/or textile fibres.

First, it is important for us adults to have an overview of paper, its history, its various uses today and its manufacture.

Grasses near the garden pond. These have been well prepared for paper-making by the sun, wind, rain and frost.

The collected paper includes egg cartons, fruit and vegetable packaging, folders, cartons, wrapping paper and much more. All this can be made into new drawing paper.

History and Production of Paper

Since ancient times, human beings have needed to record their historical and religious experiences, to seal contracts in writing, and to pass on to their descendants what they knew about the world, about crafts, the arts and so on. Various materials have been used for writing. In order to orient themselves better in the year, human beings developed calendars, carving stones with different kinds of marks and symbols.

Paper was invented about 3,000 years ago by the Chinese. Before this, people used papyrus made from the pulp of papyrus plant stalks. This was pressed and cemented together to produce sheets up to 130 feet (40m) long. Scraped animal skins and wax, clay and stone tablets were also used.

— Making paper

Paper is made from plant fibres that are matted together. Compressed mats that are $1/100$ of an inch (0.3 mm) thick are called paper. Thicker mats are called paper board or cardboard. Today almost all production is by machine and it uses the following raw materials:

Genuine papyrus

* *Textile waste:* rags of linen, hemp, cotton etc., when used for making paper, are sorted, cleaned, shredded, cooked with lime or bicarbonate of soda and bleached with chlorine. This results in high quality paper.

* *Cellulose:* through the chemical treatment of wood, straw, alfalfa etc., pure cellulose is produced. Cellulose doesn't yellow; therefore, when mixed with textile fibres, it's an excellent material for making paper. Mixed with wood pulp, the cellulose is used to make wrapping paper and newspaper.

* *Wood pulp:* through the mechanical slurring of various soft woods (fir and spruce), wood pulp is produced. It is used to make coarse

79

paper and corrugated cardboard. It has a tendency to yellow quickly and to be brittle.

✿ *Recycled paper:* soaking and shredding old paper produces a new and valuable raw material. Printer's ink is very hard to get out, so such paper is used to make coloured paper and cardboard.

Out of the natural fibres of wood, cloth rags and plants — and recently also out of synthetic and glass fibres — a clean, homogeneous brew containing about 1 part fibre to 100 to 200 parts water results. This is treated with fulling agents such as chalk, lime, talc, gypsum and kaolin. The fulling agents serve to fill out the pores of the fibrous material, increase the strength of the paper and make the paper whiter, heavier, easier to print on and less expensive. The lime, for example, strengthens the paper mat or felt, makes the paper smooth and shiny and makes it hold the black and coloured inks better.

In long sieve machines, the liquid mix of fibres is continuously shaken to thicken it by removing water. It is then matted, felted, pressed and finally rolled between hard rubber cylinders into thin sheets. Then it is cut and rolled on cylinders.

The watermarks that are on many papers are produced by patterns on the flat metal sieves.

The finished paper can be coated, infused or pressed again and thus becomes a higher quality product.

⌐ *Types of paper*

✿ *High quality paper:* hand-made paper, paper for currency, photography paper, drawing paper, cigarette paper

✿ *Writing paper:* envelope paper, book paper, typewriter and writing paper

✿ *Printing paper:* paper for Bibles, paper for prints of illustrations and paintings, newsprint, brochure paper.

✿ *Wrapping paper:* wallpaper, paper shopping bags, toilet paper, tissue paper, parchment paper

✿ *Heavy paper:* insulation paper, Manila envelopes, heavy crepe paper

⌐ *Paper recycling*

Paper manufacturing requires large amounts of water, energy and raw materials such as wood, cellulose and old paper. Various environmental problems arise involving the heavy consumption of fresh water, wood and energy, the need for purification of runoff water, and disposal of paper. If one compares the total energy use involved in producing cellulose-free paper from fibre only, paper from wood pulp only, and paper from recycled paper, it is clear that recycled paper involves the least expenditure of energy. The water runoff and the use of fresh water is less than with paper based on cellulose. Also, this saves trees and reduces the total use of paper.

The use of paper is increasing steadily all over the world, particularly in the industrialized nations. It was expected that computers would reduce the volume of paper used, but that has not been the case. A great deal of paper is used unnecessarily in both homes and offices. The growing flood of advertising and packaging has caused paper to be a throwaway product. Most papers for print and office use are extremely short-lived and have little recycled content.

Long ago, paper was re-used as a raw material for papier-mâché. With modern de-inking processes, used paper can now more easily be made into high quality recycled paper with a 60–70% level of whiteness. Environmental paper with a grayish color is produced from unprinted paper left over from the production of paper products. We need to be conscious of our use of paper, limit it as much as possible, and use recycled paper whenever appropriate.

Making Paper with Children

Making paper is above all a watery business! For that reason, we need a room with a waterproof floor and with furniture that cannot be easily damaged. A spacious kindergarten washroom, a recreation hall, the school kitchen or a clear area in the garden would serve well. If you work outside at this time of year, you can fill the pulp vat with warm water, which will make the work very pleasant and ensure that the children will not get cold hands.

⌐ Necessary materials

- ✿ a varied collection of paper: flyers, egg cartons, packing paper, newspapers and much more
- ✿ a three-gallon (10 litre) bucket
- ✿ a quart/litre measure
- ✿ a pulp vat: a wash tub, a large dishwashing pan, or a large rectangular plastic storage container with a cover
- ✿ for each child: a cloth made of cotton, felt or fleece that is slightly larger than the pulp frames

Usually the children react with disbelief when you tell them they can make egg cartons, corrugated cardboard and used wrapping paper into smooth drawing paper

- ✿ a sponge
- ✿ pulp frames consisting of a flat sieve in a frame. A large round wire sieve used in the kitchen to extract oil from spray can be used, as can sturdy window screening cut to size
- ✿ a kitchen blender or eggbeater
- ✿ textile remnants (rags and thread from natural textiles such as linen, cotton, wool or hemp)
- ✿ dried plants and dried plant fibres
- ✿ a stirring stick or kitchen spoon
- ✿ a drying rack or clothesline
- ✿ boards for pressing
- ✿ a lot of absorbent newspaper
- ✿ two fairly large clamps
- ✿ cleaning rags, scrubbing brushes and a bucket for the floor.

Tip: for carrying paper pulp that is still wet, we recommend old newspapers and brochures.

Equipment needed for making paper with children: pulp vat, kitchen blender, eggbeater, round and rectangular sieves, cotton cloths, sponges, a rolling pin and a lot of old paper.

To introduce the children to all the things that are to be used, we play a little game. All the items are laid out in an orderly circle. Each child in turn, with eyes closed, picks up an item which he or she then explains to the group.

— Instructions

Collecting the used paper

We start off with a collection of paper. It's amazing what you can find. If we separate things according to their use, we get an idea of the many categories of paper there are: packaging, writing paper, drawing paper, painting paper, book paper, newspapers, brochures and so on.

Sorting

First we take out the things that can be used again, such as paper bags, cardboard boxes and re-usable envelopes, and put them aside.

Then we take out all paper that is covered with black print. Too much printer's ink makes it impossible to give the paper a clear colour.

Removing synthetics

Remove all paper that has glue or a self-sealing band on it, or has staples or fasteners.

Reducing the size of the pieces

The next step in the process is to reduce all the paper to coin-sized pieces.

This rather noisy work tells us a lot — through the senses of touch, hearing and sight — about the structure of different kinds of paper. The children can play guessing games, closing their eyes and trying to decide what type of paper is being ripped up. The children spur each other on, especially when many sit in a circle around a mountain of paper and there are many containers nearby for the little pieces of paper.

Tip: If you need a large quantity of old paper for a festival or large gathering when many children will be making paper, ask at your local city hall. There is usually a large amount of paper available that has been put through a paper shredder. Such paper is very good for paper-making.

Soaking

Pour water over the paper that has been torn into small pieces and let it soak for one day.

Tip: When you make a large amount of paper at a festival, soak very thin paper in warm water for just two hours and it will be ready for use.

Further reduction of the paper size

Break down the old paper by putting it, in small portions, in a kitchen blender. The finer the paper mix, the more homogenous the end product will

The dipping frames are held horizontally when they are taken out of the pulp vat and are shaken gently back and forth so that the water runs off

The dipped sheet of paper is carefully turned upside down onto the fleece cloth. Excess water is removed with a sponge.

be. If you want to maintain certain patterns or colours from the used paper, it should not be broken up too much.

It is also possible to soak different types of paper in separate containers to reduce them in size to varying degrees. For example, egg cartons and corrugated cardboard can be very finely "puréed," while used gift wrap can be left larger in size so the colour is retained.

Plant ingredients

Soak dried grasses, leaves or pressed flowers for about half an hour and put them in the pulp vat at the end.

Textile ingredients

Material from cotton, wool and linen remnants should be put in at the very end.

The dipping frame is carefully removed and the sheet of dipped paper remains on the cotton under-cloth

Finally the cloth with the dipped paper is hung on the drying stand

Preparation of the pulp mixture

The pulp mixture is prepared in a large, low container, a dishwashing pan or clothes-washing tub. A large plastic storage container with a tight fitting lid is also well suited. As a general guideline, put in about 10 quarts (10 litres) of water to 1 quart (1 litre) of pulp mixture. Other proportions will also work and you'll need to experiment to find what

works best for you with each particular batch of paper. Now add the plant and textile ingredients.

Dipping the paper

On top of a pile of newspaper next to the pulp vat, we put the cotton or felt cloth and smooth it out. The dipping frame is placed so that the sieve is on top and is covered by the frame.

Making and folding an envelope

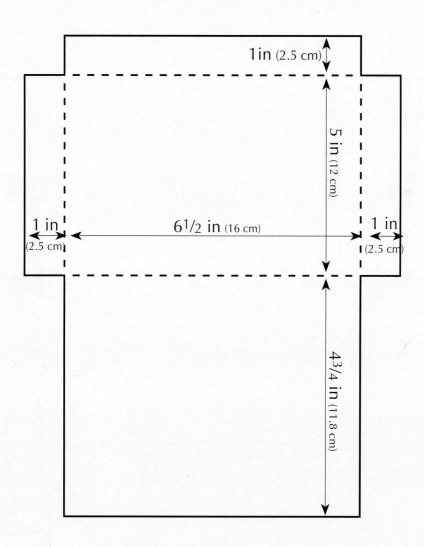

1 in (2.5 cm)

5 in (12 cm)

1 in
(2.5 cm)

6¹/₂ in (16 cm)

1 in
(2.5 cm)

4³/₄ in (11.8 cm)

Before we dip the frame we stir the paper mixture vigorously with a ladle or a kitchen spoon.

The frame is put vertically into the vat at the far side and is then drawn towards the body; it is then turned to the horizontal and carefully lifted out of the water. Gently shake the frame back and forth to distribute the paper evenly on the sieve and let the water run off.

After the water has run off, carefully lift the frame. Put one corner of the sieve frame on the lower edge of the cloth and tip the frame over very carefully, depositing the paper onto the cloth. Press gently on the frame so that much of the water is absorbed by the underlying layer of newspapers. Careful sponging can speed up this process.

Drying

Put another cloth and several sheets of newspaper on the newly dipped sheet and the fleece underlayer, and compress the whole pile with a rolling pin.

Tip: several sheets can be dried at once by stacking them with their fleece cloths and newspaper sheets between two flat pieces of wood, holding them together with clamps. The newspaper soaks up a lot of water so the drying process is greatly accelerated.

Now the cloth with the newly dipped sheet is hung out to dry on the line. When the sheet is fully dry — usually after about two days — it is separated from the cloth and ironed between two sheets of newspaper.

Tip: if there is not enough time to dry the paper, the wet sheets can be placed on newspaper and carefully carried home by the children.

Painting and handicrafts without toxic chemicals

Suggestions by Gudrun Obermann

The activities in this section go well with the paper-making project. They should motivate teachers who do crafts with children to begin to use natural, poison-free adhesives. Through this, the children come into contact with materials that are not harmful to their health and that are also friendly to the environment. The suggestions can help teachers become involved in working in a natural way. They are meant especially for children who, for one reason or another, cannot work outdoors. This includes children who are bedridden and children who, because of severe disabilities, cannot go outdoors regularly. Many of the following projects can be done on a table or even on a bed.

With natural materials such as twigs from trees and bushes, fruit, seashells, sand, stone, bark and so on, children can be extremely creative. These materials should not be glued together with the conventionally-available glues that contain solvents and preservatives. You can either make your own glue or dispense with glue entirely or use other ways of joining things, such as with string or mesh.

The following projects use harmless natural substances. These involve no synthetic, poisonous solvents, preservatives or dyes. The dyes are derived from plants (see *Spring* in this book series).

You don't need solvents because the colours and the adhesives used are all water soluble. Preservatives are not used because they are also unnecessary. The quantities are small and they are quickly used up.

Finally, you can usually find other ways of holding things together — for example, tied with wool yarn, wire, cord, grass, straw and so on. When this is not possible, there are always non-toxic alternatives such as dough or nails. Whenever you want to join two things, ask yourself if it is possible to do the job with nails or by tying instead of with adhesives. As an example, see the following projects for building two musical instruments and a little windmill.

Have a good time trying out these suggestions.

Paste and Plaster

Many natural materials can be joined with adhesives like paste and plaster. Light-weight objects such as leaves, grass, moss and feathers can be held together or attached to a sheet of paper with paste. Paste, for example, will hold grains of sand on a piece of paper to create a beautiful landscape (see page 90). If you add natural colouring to the paste, it can be used for finger painting (see page 88). Heavy materials, such as stones, seashells, twigs and fruit, hold together with a homemade dough or plaster material (see page 67 for a recipe for homemade beeswax plaster).

Sand landscapes are made using coloured sand, leaves, moss and fruits

Glue

Preparation: For the adhesive, use a granular powder called methyl cellulose. It works well in craft projects and is totally non-toxic. It can be purchased in building supply stores or in stores specializing in ecological building materials. Put a teaspoon of the powder in a glass jar and mix it with 2 ounces (50 ml) of cold water. In thirty minutes, the paste is ready to be used.

By adding water, you can change the adhesive properties to suit the job at hand. Because it contains no preservatives, use it up as soon as possible. It will keep in the refrigerator for one to two weeks.

Finger-Painting

Mix and stir the paste with coloured water. The coloured water can be made from a powder or by decoction. For the powder, cut up the various plant materials — leaves, stems, bark and fruits — and mash them with a mortar and pestle. Decoction is similar to making tea: put the pieces of plant that are to provide the colour into hot water. The water becomes coloured and the plant material can be strained out. Take two tablespoons of this coloured liquid, add 2 ounces (50 ml) of water, and pour this into a jar. Mix the water and colour well and then add one teaspoon of paste. The intensity of the plant colour depends on the strength of the decoction and how much it has been diluted. In half an hour, the paste has thickened enough to be used for finger painting. It will keep in the refrigerator for one to two weeks.

Colours

* *green,* stinging nettles or spinach leaves:
  Mash 4 ounces (100 g) of fresh nettles or spinach leaves and boil in 2 ounces (50 ml) of water.

Allow to steep for one hour and then remove the leaves. The brew is ready to be used as a dye.

❀ *brown,* black tea or the brown outer leaves of an onion:
Take the brown leaves from four or five onions, mix with 2 ounces (50 ml) of water and bring to the boil. Allow to steep until the water turns brown.

❀ *red,* beetroot juice:
Cook red beetroots and keep the water.

❀ *blue,* blueberry juice:
Pass the fresh blueberries through a sieve.

❀ *violet:* elderberry juice

❀ *yellow,* powdered saffron or decoction of sorrel:
For a yellow colour, make a decoction of the coloured mignonette using about 4 ounces (100 g). A half-teaspoon of saffron powder mixed with 2 ounces (50 ml) of water will also work well.

An advantage of homemade finger paints is that you not only create the colour and determine its intensity, but you can also vary the thickness of the paint. If the paint is too thin, you need only pour in a bit of paste and wait until it has thickened. If it is too thick, you can thin it with water or with some of the coloured liquid. Besides, you know that these homemade paints contain only non-toxic, natural substances and therefore can be given to the children without worry. A pleasant side effect of home-made paints is the lovely fresh smell they have.

A disadvantage is that the colours are not very intense. You should use a piece of bright white heavy paper or a white bed sheet as a background rather than a piece of window glass. Also, dilute the coloured decoction or the powder as little as possible.

Sand Pictures

First sift the sand — obtained from the beach, a building supply centre or elsewhere — through a large kitchen sieve to remove stones and plant material. Catch the sand in a bucket and then put it into jars. Now the colouring can begin. Use the same coloured fluids used to make finger paints (see above). For example, the juice of spinach or nettles is used to make green sand.

The sand must be thoroughly soaked with the coloured water, juice or dye. Mix the coloured fluid with the sand in the jars using a spoon. Then spread it on newspaper and let it dry outside. It can be put back into jars and, if thoroughly dried and stored in a dark place, it will keep for several years. Naturally-coloured sandy soil (ranging from black to dark brown to light brown) can be sieved and stored in jars. This can add natural brown tones to the picture. A sandy soil is better than a loamy soil, since it consists mostly of quartz crystals that can work well for sand painting.

You can also collect assorted nuts (acorns, birch seeds and so on), seashells, twigs, leaves and moss. After being dried, all of these will keep well and can be used in their dried state.

A landscape can be "painted" using the sands of different colours and the collected natural materials. Apply a brushful of paste onto a large sheet of paper. The sand will stick to the damp streak of paste when it is gently sprinkled on. If the paper is picked up and gently shaken, the

Sand landscapes

loose grains of sand will roll onto the paste. Each colour should be applied with a separate application of paste onto the paper. Apply new paste to a new section of paper and use a different colour material so that the colours aren't mixed.

After the application of the sand, the loose grains of sand remaining on the surface of the paper can be shaken into a glass container and used later for special colour effects. Then the other materials that have been collected can be pasted onto the paper. Special effects can be created with larger stones, seashells and plant fibres.

Variations: instead of a large piece of paper, you can use a blank greeting card or a piece of folded paper. An area is marked off and brushed with paste and then sprinkled with sand. Other materials can be also pasted on. Unique greeting cards and cards for special occasions such as birthdays and holidays can be created in this way.

The colour of the sand will fade over time from exposure to sunlight. The sand can be coloured again and used to make another picture.

90

Unique greeting cards can be made with coloured sand

Castanets and pan pipes

Nature Mobile

Attach various natural objects to a tree branch. These can vary according to the time of year.

❀ In spring, bright ribbons, a hazelnut twig in flower, feathers and little animals cut from wood can be hung on the branch.

❀ In summer, you can use seashells, dried flowers and holiday mementos.

❀ In autumn, use nuts, leaves of different colours and feathers.

❀ In winter, you might decorate the branch with ivy, evergreens, straw stars, bright ribbons and assorted nuts (acorns, pine cones, sycamore seed balls and so on).

Pan Pipes

Pan pipes can be made out of a piece of bamboo about $4^1/2$ feet (1.5m) long. The inner diameter of the bamboo tube should be about $7/16$ inch (1 cm). If there is still soft matter in the tube it must be scraped out with a long thin metal rod or a knife. Saw the bamboo into five to eight pieces. The first piece should be at least 2 inches (5 cm) long. Each additional piece should be $7/16$ inch (1 cm) longer than the previous one.

Although a length of bamboo is hollow, it does have thickened joints, called nodes. At these joints the tube is blocked. When the bamboo is sawn into pieces, the joints should be retained so that each tube of the pan pipe has an open end and a closed end.

The last piece of tube should be about five inches (13 cm) long. Each tube must then be well sanded on the outside with a piece of fine sandpaper, to remove all the sharp edges. Tie the pipes together tightly, in order of length, with a piece of strong cord just below the open end. Then tie together the other ends with another length of cord. When you blow over the open end of the pipes, the individual notes sound.

Castanets

To make castanets you need two wooden spoons. Saw off the handles of the spoons but leave about 3/4 inch (1.5 cm) just above the bowl of the spoon. Smooth away the saw marks with sandpaper and drill a hole in the handle of each spoon. Tie the two pieces together with a piece of coloured yarn or string so that the two hollow sides of the spoon face each other. The castanets can be coloured with finger paints.

Pinwheel

Materials: four feathers of equal size, a bottle cork, a knife, a hand drill, a nail $1\frac{1}{2}$ inches (4 cm) long, two small wooden beads, a hammer, a stick.

For the pinwheel you need four feathers of equal length from a pigeon, chicken, seagull or other bird. Cut off a piece of bottle cork about $\frac{7}{16}$ inch (1 cm) long. Drill a hole through the middle of the cork. In the outer surface of the cork, drill four equally spaced holes opposite each other. One feather will be stuck in each hole. Then thread one bead on the nail; pass the nail through the cork, and thread the other bead onto the nail. Then hammer the nail into one end of a sturdy stick $\frac{1}{2}$ to 1 inch (1–2 cm) in diameter. Finally, put the feathers into the holes.

Stand the stick up in a flower bed or a flower box and it will turn in the wind.

The Children's Nature and Garden Centre

The Children's Nature and Garden Centre in Reichshof is open to all and offers seasonal nature classes. The Centre works closely with kindergartens and schools, and with parents. Its grounds are well equipped for practical, hands-on workshops, seminars and extended courses, and it also offers advice and support for those who want to set up similar schemes elsewhere.

For more information, contact the Centre at:

Natur-Kinder-Garten-Werkstatt Reichshof
Dorner Weg 4
51580 Reichshof
Germany

Tel.: +49-22 61-52 22 1

Further Reading

Adolphi, Sybille, *Making Fairy Tale Scenes,* Floris Books, Edinburgh.

—, *Making Flower Children,* Floris Books, Edinburgh

—, *Making More Flower Children,* Floris Books, Edinburgh.

Aeppli, Willi, *Care and Development of the Human Senses,* Steiner Press, London.

Anschütz, Marieke, *Children and their Temperaments,* Floris Books, Edinburgh.

Barz, Brigitte, *Festivals with Children,* Floris Books, Edinburgh.

Berger, Petra, *Feltcraft,* Floris Books, Edinburgh.

Berger, Thomas, *The Christmas Craft Book,* Floris Books, Edinburgh.

Berger, Thomas & Petra, *Crafts through the Year,* Floris Books, Edinburgh.

—, *The Gnome Craft Book,* Floris Books, Edinburgh.

Clouder, Chris & Martyn Rawson, *Waldorf Education,* Floris Books, Edinburgh.

Crossley, Diana, Muddles, *Puddles and Sunshine,* Hawthorn Press, Stroud.

Dancy, Rahima Baldwin, *You are your Child's First Teacher,* Celestial Arts.

Evans, Russell, *Helping Children to Overcome Fear,* Hawthorn Press, Stroud.

Grunelius, Elisabeth, *Early Childhood Education and the Waldorf School Plan,* Waldorf Monographs, New York.

Guéret, Frédérique, *Magical Window Stars,* Floris Books, Edinburgh.

Harwood, A.C. *The Way of a Child,* Steiner Press, London.

Jaffke, Freya, *Work and Play in Early Childhood,* Floris Books, Edinburgh & Anthroposophic Press, New York.

Jenkinson, Sally, *The Genius of Play,* Hawthorn Press, Stroud.

König, Karl, *The First Three Years of the Child,* Floris Books, Edinburgh.

Kornberger, Horst, *The Power of Stories,* Floris Books, Edinburgh.

Kutsch, Irmgard and Brigitte Walden, *Autumn Nature Activities for Children,* Floris Books, Edinburgh.

—, *Spring Nature Activities for Children,* Floris Books, Edinburgh.

—, *Summer Nature Activities for Children,* Floris Books, Edinburgh.

—, *Winter Nature Activities for Chidren,* Floris Books, Edinburgh.

Kraul, Walter, *Earth, Water, Fire and Air,* Floris Books, Edinburgh.

Leeuwen, M van & J Moeskops, *The Nature Corner,* Floris Books, Edinburgh.

Mellon, Nancy, *Storytelling with Children,* Hawthorn Press, Stroud.

Meyer, Rudolf, *The Wisdom of Fairy Tales,* Floris Books, Edinburgh.

Muller, Gerda, *Autumn* (a board book), Floris Books, Edinburgh.

Müller, Brunhild, *Painting with Children,* Floris Books, Edinburgh.

Neuschütz, Karin, *Sewing Dolls,* Floris Books, Edinburgh.

Oldfield, Lynne, *Free to Learn,* Hawthorn Press, Stroud.

Petrash, Carol, *Earthwise: Environmental Crafts and Activities with Young Children,* Floris Books, Edinburgh & Gryphon House, Maryland.

Rawson, Martyn & Michael Rose, *Ready to Learn,* Hawthorn Press, Stroud.

Reinckens, Sunnhild, *Making Dolls,* Floris Books, Edinburgh.

Santer, Ivor, *Green Fingers and Muddy Boots,* Floris Books, Edinburgh.

Schmidt, Dagmar & Freya Jaffke, *Magic Wool,* Floris Books, Edinburgh.

Sealey, Maricristin, *Kinder Dolls,* Hawthorn Press, Stroud.

Steiner, Rudolf, *The Education of the Child in the Light of Anthroposophy,* Steiner Press, London, & Anthroposophic Press, New York.

Taylor, Michael, *Finger Strings,* Floris Books, Edinburgh.

Thomas, Anne & Peter, *The Children's Party Book,* Floris Books, Edinburgh

Wolck-Gerche, Angelika, *Creative Felt,* Floris Books, Edinburgh.

—, *More Magic Wool,* Floris Books, Edinburgh.

—, *Papercraft,* Floris Books, Edinburgh.

Sources for Natural Materials

Australia
Morning Star
www.morningstarcrafts.com.au
Winterwood Toys
www.winterwoodtoys.com.au

North America
The Waldorf Early Childhood Association of North America maintains an online list of suppliers at: www.waldorfearlychildhood.org/sources.asp

UK
Myriad Natural Toys
www.myriadonline.co.uk

Waldorf Schools

In 2010 there are almost 1000 Waldorf schools and 1,500 kindergartens in over 60 countries around the world. Up-to-date information can be found on any of the websites below.

Australia
Association of Rudolf Steiner Schools in Australia, PO Box 111, Robertson, NSW 2577
rssa@bigpond.com
www.steineroz.com

New Zealand
Federation of Rudolf Steiner Schools, PO Box 888, Hastings, Hawkes Bay
waldorf@voyager.nz
www.rudolfsteinerfederation.org.nz

North America
Association of Waldorf Schools of North America, 3911 Bannister Road, Fair Oaks, CA 95628
awsna@awsna.org
www.whywaldorfworks.org

South Africa
Southern African Federation of Waldorf Schools, PO Box 280, Plumstead 7801
federation@waldorf.org.za
www.waldorf.org.za

UK
Steiner Schools Fellowship, Kidbrooke Park, Forest Row, RH18 5JB
mail@swsf.org.uk
www.steinerwaldorf.org.uk